Chicago Bird & Cage Co.

ILLUSTRATED CATALOGUE

Birds, Cages and Supplies

RETRO PEACOCK EDITION
INTRODUCTION by R. PEACOCK

"The Largest Mail Order House of Its Kind in Chicago"

MANUFACTURERS - IMPORTERS - WHOLESALERS - RETAILERS

Published in 2012 by Retro Peacock Books
Toronto, Canada
www.RetroPeacock.com

This book was originally published as an illustrated catalogue circa 1930 by The Chicago Bird and Cage Company of Chicago, Illinois.

To stay informed about upcoming Retro Peacock editions, please visit www.RetroPeacock.com.

No part of the contents of this publication may be reproduced or used in any form or by any means—graphic, electronic, or mechanical, including photocopying, recording, or information storage-and-retrieval systems—without the written permission of the publisher.

© 2012 Retro Peacock Books
All rights reserved

Printed in the United States of America

First edition

ISBN-13: 978-0986863707
ISBN-10: 098686370X

INTRODUCTION

Dear Reader,

Indulging in mementos of the past can be a magical experience which brings a certain yearning a foregone world which is fanciful and free of the intricacies of modern life. Consider, for example, a time as recently as the turn of the twentieth century when people lived in a world where wild birds and exotic animals were thought of as abundantly available commodities to be freely kept as pets. These animals were commodified to such an extent that one could open up a mail-order catalogue and select pets sold under trademarked brand names. Buying a pet was as easy and as routine as browsing through a catalogue for furniture, toys, and items for the home.

In fact, there were many intriguing companies which sold pets to consumers using the mail-order model of business. In the 1930s, one major distribtor situated in the windy city was known as **Chicago Bird & Cage Company**. Self-touted as the "The Largest Mail Order House of its Kind in Chicago," this company had a wide geographic reach given its strategic location in Chicago, the largest railway hub in the world at that time. In fact, their shipping method was so robust that the company guaranteed live shipments of animals at any distance in the United States, Canada, and Mexico in any season.

This book offers fascinating glimpse of the many birds and other exotic fancy which were available as pets to all who could afford them. Offerings from Chicago Bird and Cage Co. were highlighted by their signature lines of parrots, including the specially bred Mexican "Parrot With The Human Voice" and "Pirate Red Head Parrot," both guaranteed to learn to talk. Beyond these, the company offered a wide selection of locally-sourced and imported bird cages and supplies, as well as a menagerie of other exotic creatures available for order, including Brazilian Cardinals, and even Marmozette Monkeys ("The smallest monkey in existence")!

This high-quality edition is an unabridged replication of the original catalogue produced circa 1930, using a rare original source copy. **Retro Peacock** is dedicated to producing fine quality art and photo editions of ornithological ephemera utilizing modern digital imaging methods, and all of our editions have been expertly processed to capture all the details of the original. Every tiny stroke of the many etchings included in this volume has been detailed and reproduced. Recreated using technology far superior to any available in the 1930s, this catalogue is printed and optimized for maximal quality and longevity in a format that captures the appearance of the original catalogue when first printed.

Whether you are a pet-lover, a collector of ephemera, a historian, or an afficionado of vintage literature, this book will be an excellent addition to your collection and enable you to experience and relive what were once bygone memories of the past.

We Hope That You Will Enjoy This Book

R. Peacock
RetroPeacock.com

SUGGESTIONS TO CUSTOMERS

REQUEST—Your request for our bird catalog received and we have mailed same at the very first mailing. We trust this book will help you in keeping your pet in the best of health and to make a success when breeding canaries.

SHIPPING FACILITIES—Chicago is the largest railroad center in the world, so quick shipments can be made to any town in the United States and Canada as we are daily shipping to customers on the Atlantic and Pacific coasts.

WHAT WE GUARANTEE—That all birds and fish which we ship will reach your express office alive. That your order will be filled promptly and everything is fully as good as represented.

WEATHER CONDITIONS do not affect shipping as our approved method of packing enables us to ship birds, fish, etc., any distance in the United States, Canada and Mexico with perfect safety.

TESTING—We test the voice of every male canary before shipment is made and examine every bird and pet to be sure they are in perfect health and condition.

SMALL ORDERS—We take as much pains to fill small orders promptly and correctly as we do larger ones; therefore do not hesitate to order what you want if it only amounts to a small **order**

OUR PRICES—Our constant aim is to put our prices as low as good reliable merchandise can be sold. On any large order we will gladly quote you our lowest figures.

HOW TO PAY—Send Post Office money order, bank draft, express money order, registered letter, or personal check at our risk. A 25% deposit is required on all C. O. D. shipments.

EXPRESS CHARGES on birds, fish and all goods listed in this catalog are to be paid by the purchaser. Should you order a large amount of bird seed or other heavy supplies, it will be much cheaper to ship them by freight instead of express.

OUR CATALOG—Lay this catalog away in a safe place! Refer to it for all particulars, but if you wish some information not found in this book please write us. When you send us your order we will try to give you good values and complete satisfaction.

SPECIAL BULLETIN—This is a bulletin issued frequently and contains up-to-the-minute information. At any time you wish a new bulletin it will be forwarded on request. It will keep you posted and save you money.

"HI-GRADE" stands for quality and if any merchandise reaches you that is not satisfactory, kindly inform us at once and we will give your letter immediate attention.

TIME PAYMENT PLAN
Order Now—Pay Later

We will hold for you any birds and cages you select. Pay one-quarter down and the balance in installments as convenient, even as low as one dollar. We make shipment of your complete order when last payment is completed. We specialize on canaries only and in this way you obtain birds without shrill notes, discords, or lice.

OUR PARROTS ARE GUARANTEED TO LEARN TO TALK

"The Parrot With The Human Voice"
The Kind That Learn To Talk Any Language

"THE HUMAN VOICE PARROT"
OUR OWN SPECIAL IMPORTED AND SELECTED GENUINE MEXICAN DOUBLE YELLOW HEADED PARROTS

Their talking ability is unlimited. They are large sized birds of a beautiful bright green plumage, with red tipped wings, red and blue feathers in wings and tail and yellow forehead. Our price is as follows:

The Human Voice Yellow Head Parrots **$15.00**

The Human Voice Parrots are a choice selection of Mexican Double Yellow Heads from the first breeding, which always contains the nicest plumage, healthiest and most intelligent birds. A Human Voice Parrot will always become an "Ideal Talker."

Mexican Double Yellow Head Parrots can be taught very easily **$10.00**
Mexican Double Yellow Head Parrots, extra fine selected.......... **12.50**
Mexican Double Yellow Head Parrots, already talking.............. **30.00** and up
Mexican Red Head Parrots, easily taught to talk................ **8.00**
Panama Parrots, tame and gentle...................................... **30.00**
African Gray Parrots **40.00**
Amazon Parrots **20.00**
Maracaibo Parrots **15.00**
Cuban Parrots, very tame..**10.00**

CHICAGO BIRD AND CAGE COMPANY

COLD WEATHER DOES NOT AFFECT SHIPPING   5

"A Natural Pirate Red-Head Parrot"

"THE PIRATE RED HEAD PARROT"
THESE BIRDS ARE ALL IMPORTED. BRED IN MEXICO AND ESPECIALLY TRANSPORTED TO US.

They may well be called the pet of the family. They are very quiet and gentle birds and there is much pleasure in teaching them.

The Mexican Redhead Pirate Parrots..............................$12.00

The Mexican Red Head Pirates are a very hardy and vigorous parrot and live a long time under good treatment. They learn very rapidly and become excellent whistlers and singers in addition to their talking ability.

OUR TALKING PETS
"THE EDUCATED TALKING PANAMA PARROT"

These parrots come to us through the direct connections with the biggest dealers and importers in America and our numerous agents in Mexico and Panama.

The Educated Talking Panama Parrot..........................$30.00

These parrots are tame and have a gentle disposition. Their quiet ways, together with their beautiful plumage makes them very popular. They will CRY, LAUGH, SING, TALK and WHISTLE. They also seem to be more hardy and less affected with colds and diseases than other birds.

CHICAGO BIRD AND CAGE COMPANY

TALKING PARROTS

"Polly" is as much a member of some families as a child. He is talked to by everyone and is regarded as everybody's friend. The pleasure of having a good talking parrot in the home comes as soon as you form an acquaintance with one. It is not unusual to say to a parrot: "Hello, Polly" and have him retort: "Hello, Mother," or to have him call you by your first name.

> GUARANTEE: With each parrot we give a written guarantee that it will learn to talk. This gives you opportunity to see for yourself just what the bird can do, it allows you to be your own judge, giving you six months for the test; this makes you absolutely safe. We also assure safe arrival.

THE MEXICAN YELLOW HEAD PARROT is known as one of the finest talking parrots bred. They are large, vigorous, very docile, loving disposition and altogether a most pleasing pet and companion. The body color is bright green with double spots of yellow on the head, which in time grow in size until almost the entire head and throat are yellow. Occasionally red spots are at wing points and tail with a few blue feathers also, making a very attractive bird. See how intelligent this specimen looks, on opposite page and cover. They become attached to the master or mistress of a household and talk to them as if imbued with human instincts. They have clear voices and talk plainly. We can assure you complete satisfaction when you order a Mexican Yellow Head Parrot, and each one is guaranteed to learn.

THE MEXICAN RED HEAD PARROT may be well called the pet of the family. He is very quiet and gentle bird and therefore there is much pleasure in teaching him. Their plumage is especially beautiful, having solid green bodies with touches of red at the wings. Their eyes are very bright, indicating liveliness. Many of them talk wonderfully well, others whistle, some imitate coughing, singing and generally try to mock you. They are also hardy and vigorous and live a long time under good treatment. Each one is guaranteed to learn.

HOW TO KEEP YOUR PARROT HEALTHY

COLDS—Put in warm place where temperature is about 80 to 90 degrees and use our "HI-GRADE" BIRD TONIC.

INDIGESTION—Feed parrot a plain diet of cracked corn, millet seed and padda, also have plenty of our "HI-GRADE" GRAVEL on the bottom of cage

CONSTIPATION—Feed three to six drops of Castor Oil once or twice daily, also use our "HI-GRADE" BIRD TONIC.

DIARRHEA—Caused by sour and spoiled food, keep parrot in warm place, do not feed water or green foods, but give plain dry food sprinkled with red pepper, also a little honey.

ASTHMA—The parrot should be given a change of diet with fresh fruit and fresh red peppers.

INSECTS—Dust the cage thoroughly with our "HI-GRADE" INSECT POWDER, also dust through the feathers on all parts of the parrot.

WOUNDS, BRUISES, SORE EYES, etc.—Wash sore spots and apply our "HI-GRADE" BIRD BALM.

WE HAVE ALL KINDS OF CANARIES

"THE FOUR WONDERS"
Linnet Canary—White Canary—Sunkist Chopper Canary—Top Knot Canary

LINNET CANARY
The plumage of these birds is entirely of a dark greenish color. Their song consists of sweet notes. Prices: MALES, $10.00; FEMALES, $3.00.

WHITE CANARY
The plumage of these birds is entirely white and some have patches of black. Their song consists of a Mello Tone Songster and are especially bred and selected of the best singers. Prices: MALES, $12.00; FEMALES, $5.00.

SUNKIST CHOPPER CANARY
The plumage of these birds is entirely of a yellowish color. They are bred from the finest Imported stock and their song is that of a loud warbler with a variety of odd notes. Prices: MALES, $18.00; FEMALES, $6.00.

TOP KNOT CANARY
The plumage of these birds may be had in yellow, spotted or all dark. They are wonderful singers and equal in every way to the best English Top Knots. Prices: MALES, $11.00; FEMALES, $3.25.

CHICAGO BIRD AND CAGE COMPANY

A Beautiful California Warbler in Song

OUR SPECIALTIES
CALIFORNIA BEAUTY CANARIES

Our Own Special and Selected California Canaries.

Raised and Trained for Us Exclusively by Breeders in California. Their singing ability is unlimited. They do not tweet or twitter but rather warble beautifully. The clear musical tones of these California warblers are magnificent and if you are seeking a canary that will sing constantly and warble the high notes, select a California Warbler.

California Beauty Canaries, males, in full song ...**$12.50**

California Beauty Canaries, females, for breeding **3.50**

These birds are specially selected singers from California and come in three different colors, orange and lemon yellow, green and orange yellow spotted and pure olive green. These birds are crated neatly in a wooden shipping cage.

CHICAGO BIRD AND CAGE COMPANY

A Natural Roller Singing Canary

OUR SPECIALTIES
RADIOROLL ROLLERS

THE MOST WONDERFUL CANARY IN THE WORLD

Raised and Imported from Germany Especially for Us. Sings Nights as Well as Days. The Canary with a Musical Education.

Radioroll Roller Canaries, males $10.00

Radioroll Roller Canaries, females, for breeding ... 2.50

These Radioroll Rollers are different from the regular trained rollers. Their song starts with a roll of the low notes and then warble up the scale to the very high bell tones and return to the flute notes and water warble. Their tuneful melodies remind you of the music of a rare old violin. You will make no mistake by ordering one of these magnificent pets.

CHICAGO BIRD AND CAGE COMPANY

THESE BIRDS ARE IMPORTED AND AMERICAN RAISED

Natural Pose of A Singing Canary

PRICES OF CANARIES

Hartz Mountain Canaries, in full song	$ 8.00
Hartz Mountain Canaries, females	2.00
St. Andreasburg Canaries, in full song	9.50
St. Andreasburg Canaries, females	2.25
Edel Roller Canaries, in full song	10.00
Edel Roller Canaries, females	2.50
Seifert Roller Canaries, in full song	12.00
Seifert Roller Canaries, females	3.25
Seifert Roller Canaries, selected	14.00
Campaninia Roller Canaries, in full song	15.00
Campaninia Roller Canaries, females	3.75
Norwich Canaries, in song	15.00
Norwich Canaries, females	6.50
Manchester Warblers, in song	10.50
Manchester Warblers, females	3.00
Scotch Fancy Canaries, in full song	10.50
Scotch Fancy Canaries, females	3.00
Yorkshire Canaries, in full song	15.00
Yorkshire Canaries, females	6.50
Cinnamon Canaries, in full song	15.00
Cinnamon Canaries, females	6.00
California Beauty Canaries, in full song	12.50
California Beauty Canaries, females	3.50
Radioroll Roller Canaries, in full song	10.00
Radioroll Roller Canaries, females	2.50

CHICAGO BIRD AND CAGE COMPANY

A BIRD IN YOUR HOME IS A JOY FOREVER 11

A COMPLETE STOCK OF ALL VARIETIES

Our stock of these beautiful, feathered songsters is one of the most complete in America. Through our connections with German representatives, we secure the most wonderful specimens of singing canaries ever offered. All of the birds listed here are genuine, imported canaries. They are healthy, sturdy birds—all bred with the greatest care. Their plumage is especially attractive. Many are clear, canary yellow. Some are spotted with black, white or green. They vary in size from 4½ to 5 inches in length. These handsome songsters become great companions in a short time because of their tuneful warbling. They are easy to care for. A little food and water once each day is all that is necessary. Each bird is shipped in an individual wooden shipping cage and is provided with a supply of food and water. We ship canaries everywhere. Order one at these low prices.

HARTZ MOUNTAIN CANARIES

Genuine male birds from the Hartz Mountain region in Germany. They are strong, lively birds and are noted for their melodious voices. Their natural song is mellow, clear and full of variety. Just imagine one of these cheerful young fellows in your home, singing throughout the entire day. You can readily see how your appreciation for such a songster will increase. We make a specialty of these singers and they are the finest Hartz Mountain singers obtainable. Prices: males, **$8.00**; females, **$2.00**.

ST. ANDREASBURG CANARIES

Those persons who have been fortunate enough to visit Europe and hear the beautiful warbling of these attractive songsters in their native land, know that the genuine St. Andreasburg canaries are wonderful. With all their freshness and sweet song we import them to the United States. The clear, musical tones of these St. Andreasburg songsters are truly magnificent. You will make no mistake by ordering one of these St. Andreasburg songsters if you want to enliven your home with rich, sweet music. Prices: males, **$9.50**; females, **$2.25**.

SEIFERT ROLLER CANARIES

The lover of music will appreciate these wonderful Seifert Roller songsters because their voices call to mind the high trills and tremulos of the famous opera singers. These Seifert Rollers are also noted for their beautiful plumage. Being specially raised and specially trained, they represent the high quality which their name infers. They are used for trainers and masters and are taught to sing the bell roll, the flute notes, the water roll and the nightingale notes. To bird lovers we suggest these magnificent Seifert Rollers for song and plumage of all the canaries. Prices: males, **$12.00**; females, **$3.25**.

CAMPANINIA ROLLER CANARIES

In canary birds the very finest you can possibly obtain is a Campaninia Roller songster. These birds are raised and handled in the same way as the Seifert Roller, only they are trained for a longer period of time until they demonstrate fully their capability to reach any note within a range of octaves. We can fully recommend these birds if you want something really exceptional. Prices: males, **$15.00**; females, **$3.75**.

FEMALE ROLLER CANARIES

Many of our customers like to breed their canaries so as to have the pleasure of raising and training young songsters. We therefore carry a large number of choice female canaries which make good breeders and give splendid results. Top knots or crested females, 75 cents extra.

CHICAGO BIRD AND CAGE COMPANY

DISEASES AND THEIR REMEDIES

A great many folks have too large a heart for their birds and give them too many various kinds of delicacies, such as candy, sugar, apples, etc. Under no circumstances should you refill the seed cup after it has been filled in the morning, as this is a large enough portion for the bird for one day. The bird's health largely depends on the selection of seed and other foods, and it is therefore well to be certain that you are getting a quality product. If your pet is properly fed, supplied with fresh water daily and the cage kept clean and free from insects, you will very seldom have trouble with your bird. It is not well to have your cage hanging more than six feet from the floor, as the heat is too great higher than this, and the bird becomes drowsy and will not sing. Be certain that your bird is not in any draft. If your room is kept warm during the day and cold at night, be sure to throw a cover over the cage. When the bird is in good health, his appearance when not moulting is very sleek and smooth. When the bird puffs his feathers and is stupid, you can be sure that he is not in the best of health.

MOULTING—During this period the bird should have the best of care. The food should be specially prepared and avoid giving them sweets or warm foods and therefore we wish to call your attention to the fact that the best, quickest and surest way to keep your pet through the moulting period is to use our "HI-GRADE" MOULTING FOOD. It is also necessary to have a goodly amount of our "HI-GRADE" GRAVEL on the bottom of the cage, as they enjoy dusting themselves in it.

BRONCHITIS—The symptoms are a dry heavy cough and much difficulty in breathing. The bird should be kept warm. Our "HI-GRADE" BIRD TONIC should be given daily and we are certain that the bird will be in best of health in a short time.

CATARRH OR COLD—The symptoms are first sneezing and then sits with feathers puffed up. The bird should be removed to a warm room and all drafts excluded. The bird should be dieted on hard boiled eggs, mixed with our "HI-GRADE" EGG FOOD, also give a small portion of our "HI-GRADE" BIRD TONIC daily.

OVER GROWN CLAWS AND BEAKS—To eliminate the trimming of the bill and claws, it is well to have a piece of our "HI-GRADE" CUTTLEBONE in the cage at all times and a little of our "HI-GRADE" GRAVEL spread over the bottom of the cage.

CONSTIPATION—This is caused by improper diet and lack of bird gravel in cage. Feed sweet apple, fresh lettuce or other green foods. In several cases put one drop of castor oil in birds mouth, also put a few drops of our "HI-GRADE" BIRD TONIC in water.

LOSS OF VOICE—Birds often lose their song from some unknown cause and during moulting season. The best and quickest way to restore the bird's song is to use our "HI-GRADE" SONG RESTORER and feed our "HI-GRADE" BIRD SEED.

SCALY LEGS—Soak legs in warm water, washing with sponge, then apply our "HI-GRADE" BIRD SALVE and gently massage with fingers for three minutes. Repeat entire treatment for a few days.

CHICAGO BIRD AND CAGE COMPANY

DISEASES AND THEIR REMEDIES

SORE FEET is usually the result of too small a perch. For any bruises or trouble with the feet, it is well to bathe the feet in warm water and rub the same with our "HI-GRADE" BIRD SALVE.

SORE EYES—The best and safest way is to wash the eyes with luke warm water and give pet our "HI-GRADE" SONG RESTORER and TONIC, as the cause is internal.

BIRD LICE—If your bird is restless and continually picks his feathers, you can be sure your bird has lice. Remove the bird from the cage; wash cage thoroughly in scalding hot water and then apply our "HI-GADE" CAGE CLEANER. Then take the bird in your hand and dust the pet with our "HI-GRADE" LICE POWDER thoroughly through the feathers. By continuing this process, within a short time your bird will be relieved of the lice.

DIARRHOEA is caused by feeding in cold or foul drinking water, musty seed or too many sweet foods. This can be remedied by placing plenty of our "HI-GRADE" GRAVEL in the bottom of the cage and put a few drops of our "HI-GRADE" BIRD TONIC in the drinking water, also give the bird our "HI-GRADE" SONG RESTORER, all that the pet can eat.

ASTHMA—When your bird breathes very heavily and makes a wheezing sound, you can be certain it has asthma. Be careful that the bird is not kept in a damp room and does not catch a cold. We suggest for you to place the bird on a diet of sweet rape for a few weeks, also do not give bird a bath.

SCHEDULE FOR CARE AND FEEDING OF HEALTHY CANARIES

Canaries fed daily at a regular time and systematically do better than birds fed irregularly with no regard to food. For this reason and for your convenience and guidance, we offer the following schedule and asssure you, if adopted, will keep your bird in good health, plumage and song.

MONDAY—Feed "HI-GRADE" BIRD SEED and fresh water. Sprinkle "HI-GRADE" BIRD GRAVEL on bottom of cage. Feed "HI-GRADE" EGG and NESTLING FOOD with hard-boiled egg.

TUESDAY—Feed "HI-GRADE" BIRD SEED and fresh water. Sprinkle "HI-GRADE" BIRD GRAVEL on bottom of cage. Furnish water for bath, using either a bath dish or bath house. Clean cage while bird is taking bath.

WEDNESDAY— Feed "HI-GRADE" BIRD SEED and fresh water. Sprinkle "HI-GRADE" BIRD GRAVEL on bottom of cage. Feed "HI-GRADE" SONG RESTORER in a little treat cup.

THURSDAY—Feed "HI-GRADE" BIRD SEED and fresh water. Sprinkle "HI-GRADE" BIRD GRAVEL on bottom of cage.

FRIDAY—Feed "HI-GRADE" BIRD SEED and fresh water. Sprinkle "HI-GRADE" BIRD GRAVEL on bottom of cage. Furnish water for bath, using either bath dish or special bath house. Clean cage while bird is taking bath. Feed "HI-GRADE" SONG RESTORER in a little treat cup.

SATURDAY—Feed "HI-GRADE" BIRD SEED and fresh water. Sprinkle "HI-GRADE" BIRD GRAVEL on bottom of cage.

SUNDAY—Feed "HI-GRADE" BIRD SEED and fresh water. Sprinkle "HI-GRADE" BIRD GRAVEL on bottom of cage. Feed any one of the following you may have in the house—spinach, water cress, sweet apple, new dandelion, celery, fresh lettuce, but be sure to dry before feeding. Fasten "HI-GRADE" HEALTH BALL to cage.

CHICAGO BIRD AND CAGE COMPANY

CANARIES AND THEIR CARE

Who can help loving the birds as we watch their cheerful actions, jumping from branch to branch and listen to their pleasant twittering and to their wild burst of song. Their beautiful melody brightens the heart of every one and makes life happier for us all.

SELECTING AND BUYING

Many of our readers are located far from any large city and are therefore obliged to depend on ordering their birds to be shipped by express. It is very important to select a dealer on whom you can depend. When selecting a song bird always select it for beauty of song and not for its handsome plumage alone. We desire especially to warn our readers against purchasing canaries, parrots or other birds from bird peddlers.

CANARIES, THEIR CARE

Canaries demand attention and if they do not receive it soon cease their song. Canaries are companionable little fellows and easily tamed and will keep in song nearly the year round if made pets of and strict attention is paid to their diet. The tendency with bird owners in America is to constantly feed their cage birds delicacies such as sugar, hemp and other fattening foods which makes the birds lazy and soon causes them to lose their song.

Absolute cleanliness is the watchword in keeping and breeding canaries. Keep your bird's food, water and cage clean and provide it with fresh "HI-GRADE" BRAND GRAVEL spread on the cage floor daily. To neglect this is the sure means of inviting disease.

The food and water cups should be so arranged as to be easy of access for the bird's head, while the bathing dish should be shallow and still large enough to prevent the bird injuring its plumage in his vigorous plunges. The cage perches should be about twice the diameter of a common lead pencil as small perches are a source of constant misery to the birds.

THE SEED TO FEED

A bird's health and song depends on the selection of seed. Our superior "HI-GRADE" BRAND BIRD SEED consists of strictly pure Sicily Canary and sweet German Rape. We furnish this at 20 cents per box or 3 pounds for 50c. As you value the life, health and song of your bird, do not feed it the cheap mixed seed found in packages in most stores. It is usually old, of the poorest quality and frequently wormy. As an occasional treat, take one hard-boiled egg, chopped fine and mixed thoroughly until it becomes paste-like, with about the same quantity of cracker crumbs. Flavor strongly with cayenne pepper. Feed this in small quantities only. This is also a good food for young birds. A piece of apple or lettuce leaves will be enjoyed occasionally, but give them no cake, sugar, figs, etc. The cage should at all times be supplied with a piece of cuttlebone and plenty of our "HI-GRADE" BRAND BIRD GRAVEL for the bottom of the cage.

SONG RESTORER

To give your bird a change of diet and a "touch of freedom" twice or three times a week, feed your canary bird a teaspoonful of our "HI-GRADE" BRAND SONG RESTORER. They will relish it immensely, as it contains the food of the field and forests. Fresh lettuce in season, or apple should be given them occasionally.

CHICAGO BIRD AND CAGE COMPANY

CANARY BREEDING
Interesting, Educational and Amusing

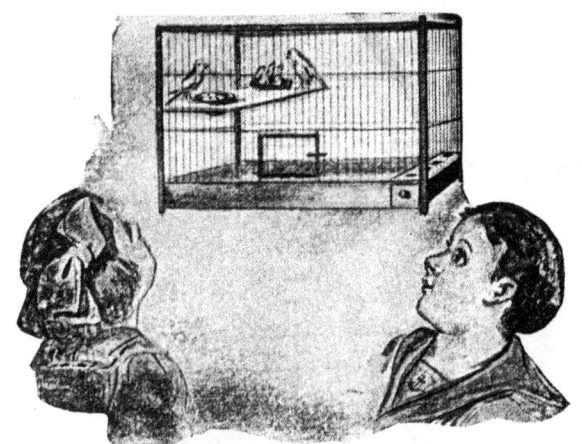

This will explain just what can be done with a pair of our wonderful canaries. The breeding of canaries is a very interesting and we may say fascinating process. It affords great pleasure to rear a nest of beautiful birds and you are always interested in watching the nest building, seeing the patience of the mother bird during the setting season, noticing the hatching and daily growth of the young birds and their development in song.

The breeding of canaries is an employment for ladies which is both PLEASANT and PROFITABLE. It is safe to say that if care is taken to follow a few simple directions which we furnish, success may be assured to all.

The usual season for mating is during December, January, February, March, April, May and June. In breeding canaries you should first choose a breeding cage which should not be less than eight inches wide and twelve inches long. The female should be placed in the breeding cage and hung within sight of your singer. If they call each other and appear to be friendly, the male should be placed with her in the breeding cage.

The breeding cage should be hung about eight feet high, against the wall in a position where it will not swing or be disturbed. Wire nests are much better than willow or other material. The bottom of the cage should be liberally strewn with our "HI-GRADE" GRAVEL and be provided with our "HI-GRADE" HAIR NESTING and the birds will arrange it in the nest to suit themselves. During the breeding season the birds should have in addition to their regular seed, a daily feed of hard-boiled egg and NESTLING FOOD, grated fine and mixed into a form of a paste; also plenty of lettuce and apple to prevent becoming egg bound. Keep plenty of fresh water and cuttlebone in the cage and try to disturb the bird as little as possible.

In about eight days after mating you may expect to find a small egg in the nest. Canaries usually lay their eggs from seven to ten o'clock in the morning and their nest usually consists of four, five or six eggs. The first eggs is usually hatched in thirteen days and then one is hatched each day. If canaries are well provided with food at all times, they will seldom eat their eggs.

After the young birds are hatched the egg and nestling food paste should be continued and the old birds will feed it to the young.

In from two to three weeks the young birds will be able to leave the nest and go about the cage and feed themselves. They should then be separated and put in another room from the parents. Soaked canary and rape seed should then be fed at this time. The parent birds are then ready for the next setting.

To the persons seeking a little PROFIT plus PLEASURE, allow us to select a beautiful pair of breeding canaries for you.

CHICAGO BIRD AND CAGE COMPANY

STRAWBERRY FINCHES—One of the smallest birds kept in captivity. They have a beautiful reddish brown plumage, with small dots, and red bill. They are very sweet singers, and their chief food consists of millet seed. Price: per pair, **$7.00**.

ZEBRA FINCHES are sociable little birds of dark grayish brown plumage, the throat, chest and breast are of a pale yellow and gray with a bright patch of orange about the middle of the body; the beak is red. These birds are quite hardy and breed in captivity. They thrive on millet seed. Price: per pair, **$7.00**.

WE HAVE BRIGHTENED MANY HOMES WITH OUR PETS 17

GRAY JAVA—A handsome bird which is especially remarkable for the neat and perfect condition in which it always keeps its plumage in the cage. The soft slate-colored body feathers are always as flat and close to the body as they can lie, the large white patches and cheeks are ever clean and the face and throat are of shiny black. The beak is bright red. They should be fed on canary and millet seed. Price: per pair, $5.00.

BLACK HEADED NUNS are very beautiful birds, their black heads forming a rich contrast with the chocolate brown bodies, and blue beaks. They are an attractive, charming bird, and of a quiet disposition. Their song is sweet and pleasing, and their food consists of canary and millet seed, but should be fed apple and green food once or twice a week. Price: per pair. $6.00.

CHICAGO BIRD AND CAGE COMPANY

FINCHES, JAVAS AND NUNS

Goldfinches, males	each	$ 6.00
Chaffinches, males	each	5.00
Chaffinches, females	each	2.50
Bullfinches, males	each	6.00
Bullfinches, females	each	5.00
Zebra Finches	per pair	7.00
Strawberry Finches	per pair	7.00
Cut Throat Finches	per pair	5.00
Nutmeg Finches	per pair	5.00
Diamond Finches	per pair	10.00
Lady Gould's Finches	per pair	20.00
Gray Javas	per pair	5.00
White Javas	per pair	12.00
Black Capped Nuns	per pair	6.00
White Headed Nuns	per pair	7.00

COCKATOOS AND MACAWS

Rose Breasted Cockatoos	each	$ 7.00
Sulphur Crest Cockatoos	each	18.00
Australian Cockatoos	each	10.00
Blue Macaws	each	30.00
Red and Blue Macaws	each	35.00

PAROQUETS

Australian Shell Paroquets—Love Birds	per pair	$ 8.00
Mexican Paroquets	per pair	7.00
Brazilian Paroquets	per pair	10.00
Bearded Paroquets	per pair	7.00
Bee Bee Paroquets	per pair	8.00
Alexander Paroquets	per pair	20.00
Yellow Shell Paroquets	per pair	12.00
Yellow Faced Paroquets	per pair	8.00

FANCY BIRDS

Blackbirds	each	$ 8.00
Mexican Red Birds	each	10.00
Mexican Mocking Birds, males	each	10.00
Mexican Mocking Birds, females	each	9.50
Japanese Robins	each	5.00
European Bullfinches, males	each	6.00
European Bullfinches, females	each	5.00
Red Cardinals, males	each	12.00
Red Cardinals, females	each	8.00
Brazilian Cardinals	each	8.50

WE BUY BIRDS, DOGS AND PETS

We handle all kinds of birds. If you have any Canaries, Parrots, Macaws, Cockatoos, or any other birds, which you would like to dispose of, write us giving full particulars in first letter. We also buy Dogs and Pets of every description.

CHICAGO BIRD AND CAGE COMPANY

A Beautiful European Goldfinch

The Goldfinch is a native of England and almost all parts of Europe. Next to the canary they may be considered the most popular cage bird. They are sought more for their beauty in the aviary and for mating with female canaries. They will live confined in a cage for 16 to 20 years. Their food consists of canary, rape and a little crushed hemp.

Price, males $6.00

LINNETS, SISKENS AND THRUSHES

	Wild	Tame
Green Linnets, males	$5.00	$10.00
Green Linnets, females	1.50	2.50
Gray Linnets, males	5.00	8.00
Gray Linnets, females	1.50	2.00
Siskens, males	$5.00	
Siskens, females	2.50	
Garrulax Thrushes	20.00	
India Shama Thrushes	20.00	
Dala Thrushes	17.50	
Gray Thrushes	9.00	
Golden Ammers	5.00	
India Green Bullbulls	17.50	

CHICAGO BIRD AND CAGE COMPANY

BRAZILIAN CARDINAL

This bird is one of the most attractive cage birds. The back is dark gray. The quill feathers of the wings are of a darker shade of the same color; the lower part of the body is grayish white and the crest is pointed like that **of the Red Cardinal.** In addition to its beautiful plumage, he is also gifted with a beautiful song. Its food consists of unhulled rice, canary seed, hemp and plenty of green food. Price, each: **$8.50**

RED CARDINAL

The Red Cardinal is one of the prettiest birds in the world. Together with its beautiful plumage this bird is gifted with a very sweet, pleasing song. It is very hardy and active, and, when properly treated, this bird often attains the age of 15 years. He is fond of canary, hemp, cracked corn and nuts. Price: male, **$12.00**; female, **$8.00**.

FROM FOREIGN COUNTRIES ONLY

OUR SPECIALTY—BIRDS, CAGES, SUPPLIES 21

A BEAUTIFUL SELECTION OF FANCY FINCHES AND RARE BIRDS
The above will give you a little idea of the beautiful fancy birds that we keep in stock during season. Kindly write and let us know what you are interested in most and we will be more than pleased to give you the desired information and prices by return mail.
NOTICE:—White Canaries are the latest public vogue.

CHICAGO BIRD AND CAGE COMPANY

OUR SPECIALTY—BIRDS, CAGES, SUPPLIES

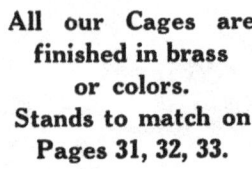

All our Cages are finished in brass or colors. Stands to match on Pages 31, 32, 33.

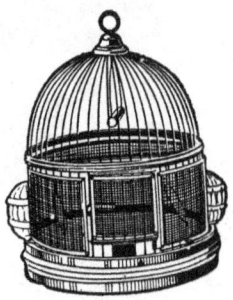

CALIFORNIA HILITE CAGE

No. 73T—Brass Cage $7.00
No. 74T—Gun Metal 7.50
No. 75T—Red 8.00
No. 76T—Blue 8.00

An all brass cage made in different finishes which makes this cage beautiful.

NEW STYLE TWO-TONE CAGE

No. 5615A—Brass only $6.75
No. 5625A—Black and Brass..... 7.25
No. 5635A—Mahogany and Brass. 7.75
No. 5645A—Brown and Brass.... 7.75
No. 5655A—Ivory and Brass..... 7.75
No. 5656A—Baby Blue and Brass 7.75

NEW POPULAR BELL DESIGN BRASS CAGE

No. 10R—Plain Brass $3.00
No. 15R—Red, Green, Blue....... 3.25

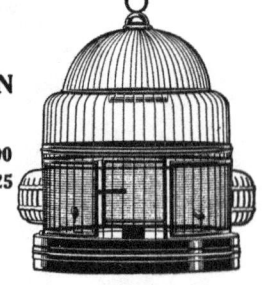

LOVE BIRD CAGE

No. 600H—12 in. Diam., 16 in. high $6.25

Exceptionally roomy, due to additional space in bottom and to cage body being higher than usual.

PURITAN HILITE CAGE

No. 615G—Brass Cage $7.00
No. 625G—Gunmetal Cage. 8.00
No. 635G—Mahogany Cage. 8.00

An all brass cage, made in different finishes.

Size 10¾ in. diam., 15 in. high.

CHICAGO BIRD AND CAGE COMPANY

THE MOST COMPLETE LINE OF CAGES 23

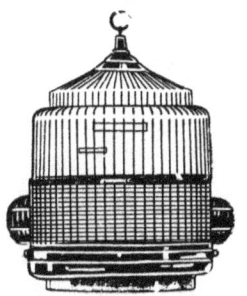

All our Cages and Stands are finished in brass or colors. Stands to match on Pages 31, 32, 33.

ORIENTAL CAGE

No. 990—Fawn $7.75
No. 991—Valley Green ... 8.00
No. 992—Heliotrope 7.75
No. 993—Evenglow 7.75
No. 994—Poinsetta 7.75
No. 995—Bluebird 8.00

ARTISTIC CAGE

No. 5301Q—Red on Brass.$9.50
No. 5302Q—Blue on Brass 9.50
No. 5303Q—Green on Brass 9.50
No. 5304Q—Black on Brass 10.00

This cage has the new style Drawer Bottom

BRASS DOME CAGES

No. 247—10¼ in. dia., 16 in. high..$3.25
No. 275—11   in. dia., 16½ in. high.. 3.75
No. 276—12   in. dia., 18 in. high.. 4.75

All brass, with guards to prevent seed from scattering; has opal seed cups.

HI-TONE CAGE

No. 5501Y—Red $5.75
No. 5502Y—Blue 5.75
No. 5503Y—Green 5.75

This Cage has the new style Drawer Bottom.

FORT DEARBORN DRAWER BOTTOM CAGE

Has new style Drawer Bottom.

No. 415—Brass and Hilite......$ 9.00
No. 425—Gunmetal and Hilite.. 10.00
No. 480—Sand 9.25
No. 481—Aszure 9.25
No. 482—French Blue 9.25
No. 483—Indian Red 9.25

CHICAGO BIRD AND CAGE COMPANY

24 WRITE FOR OUR LATEST SUCCESS, "SUNKIST CHOPPERS"

All our Cages are finished in brass or colors. Stands to match on Pages 31, 32, 33.

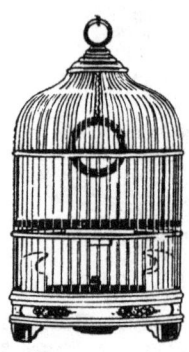

NIPON CAGE

No. 3501J—Blue .. $8.00
No. 3502J—Green   8.00
No. 3503J—Red .. 8.00

This Case has Removable Drawer Bottom.

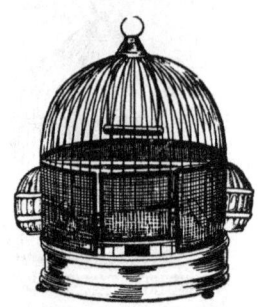

ORIOLE BRASS CAGE

No. 5600D—10 in. diam. height 14 in..... $5.00
No. 5650D — 10¾ inch diam. Height. 14½ in. 5.50

Fitted with new departure in detaching the bottom, cups, perches and swing.

FOLDING JAPANESE BUNGALOW CAGE

These cages are substantially constructed with splendid appearance; are light, airy and easy to keep clean, having movable bottoms, and are equipped with feed and water cups of beautiful china.
Price, 11½ in. x 9½ in. x 13½ in..... $3.25

DRAWER BASE CAGE

No. 75DB—Red, Green, Blue $5.75

11 inches in diameter, 14 inches high. Has removable drawer bottom.

CARLTON CAGE

No. 3275 .... $3.25

Red and black, Blue and black, Green and Black. 11 inches in diameter, 14½ inches high.

CHICAGO BIRD AND CAGE COMPANY

COLORED BUNGALOW CAGE

No. 4201MX $8.00

Beautiful two-tone colors of red, ivory, blue, gold, black. Has new removable drawer bottom for easy cleaning.

JAPANESE TOKOYO CAGE

No. 730 ....$9.75

11 inches diameter.

A very attractive cage in two-tone colors of ivory, red, blue, green. Has new removable drawer bottom for easy cleaning.

COLORED CHARM CAGE

No. 6000 ....$7.75

Beautiful new style cage in new colors of buff, green or red. Stand to match cage, $3.50 extra.

BRILLIANT COLOR CAGE

No. 1800 ....$4.00

In rich color of brilliant red, green or red. This cage is a beauty. Stand to match, $2.25 extra.

CHICAGO BIRD AND CAGE COMPANY

WE SHIP MOST OF OUR BIRDS DURING THE WINTER

IVORY DOME CAGE

No. 02225—10¼"		$4.25
No. 02226—11"		5.00
No. 02227—11¾"		5.75

Ivory Dome Cage, solid brass wire guard, trimmed in gold; opal shell cups.

SPECIAL JAPANNED CAGE

No. 165— 9½"x6½", each....$2.25
No. 166—10½"x7", each.... 2.50
No. 167—11" x7½", each.... 3.00

Fancy oblong square japanned cage. Complete with opal feed cups.

"E-Z-KLEEN"

No. 92 ....$4.25

New style removable drawer board. Large size cage in various colors of green or red, blue or orange. A real beauty for the price.

MONKEYS

Rhesus Monkeys ....$30.00 up
Java Monkeys .... 25.00 up
Ringtail Monkeys .... 25.00 up
Marmozette Monkeys 25.00
(The smallest monkey in existence.)

WHITE CANARIES

Have you seen the latest in song birds—the White Canary which are taught to sing every note they produce. A written guarantee with every canary, which means your canary must satisfy.
Males.....$12.00   Females.....$5.00

CHICAGO BIRD AND CAGE COMPANY

HIGRADE IMPORTED GERMAN CAGES

SANDAM

Cages again show the way in IMPORTED BIRD CAGES by creating and designing cages to meet the demand of the general trend towards Modernistic Designs.

The construction of these SANDAM imported bird cages are made for long wear and durability. The combination of colors are so beautifully decorated and blended so as to harmonize with its surroundings. Above all, the SANDAM imported square cages are always attractive, excellent quality, modern shapes, newest colors and most advantageous in prices.

No. 0115—12"x7⅞"x10⅞" $6.00
Highly polished brass with hand painted glass guards. Sliding drawer bottom.

No. 0221—17½"x11½" $10.00
Red, Blue, Green, Black colors. Hand painted celluloid guards. Double drawer bottoms. Blended in two-tone colors.

No. 0167—14"x8"x11" $9.00
Highly polished brass with hand painted glass guards. Sliding drawer bottom.

CHICAGO BIRD AND CAGE COMPANY

SANDAM IMPORTED BIRD CAGES

No. 0263—15½"x9"x12 ....$12.00
A real beauty. Blended in two-tone colors. Green or copper color with glass guards. Drawer bottom.

No. 0264—15½"x10½"x12½" $13.00
Beautifully decorated in colors of blue, copper or green in two-tone effect. Has double drawer bottom.

No. 0246—14½"x7½"x10½" $8.00
No. 0246½—15½"x8½"x11½" 9.00
Polished brass cage with large decorated glass guards. Double sliding bottoms.

No. 0261—15¾"x9"x12 ....$11.00
This cage is a great favorite. The harmonious colors or red and green appeal to all. Glass guards with double slide drawer.

CHICAGO BIRD AND CAGE COMPANY

SANDAM IMPORTED BIRD CAGES 29

No. 0203—14"x7½"x11" $8.50

Beautifully stippled in crystalized finishes of red, green, orange. Has Sliding drawer and glass guard on silhouette designs.

No. 0124—12¾"x8"x11".
Solid Brass $7.50
Colors 6.00

Full tubing cage, hand painted glass guards with double drawer bottom. In green and blue gold color.

No. 0105—16"x8"x12" $11.00

A beautiful large size, solid brass cage. Has cut and hand painted glass. This cage sure is a beauty.

No. 0220—15½"x9½"x12" $11.50

Highly brass cage. Porcelain cups inside cage to prevent seed from scattering. Drawer bottom. This cage is the antique style.

CHICAGO BIRD AND CAGE COMPANY

30 A BUSY SECTION OF OUR INSPECTING AND SHIPPING DEPT.

A FEW FACTS OF HOW YOUR ORDERS ARE PACKED

OUR SHIPPING DEPARTMENT.—Located in the heart of Chicago. This makes us centrally located, near the post office for early mailing and near the express office for early shipping. Weather conditions do not affect shipping as our shipping department is equipped with the most modern methods of packing, insuring safe and quick delivery. All birds are crated safely in a wooden shipping cage.

ORDER BY MAIL.—With our catalogue you really have a PET SHOP spread out before you. There are no chances to be taken, your orders receive careful attention and with the least possible delay. We strive to please and satisfy at all times and hope to make those that are buying for the first time continue as our old customers have.

SERVICE THAT IS UNEQUALLED ELSEWHERE.—Your orders are always appreciated regardless of being small or large, and can assure you service and prompt shipments on all orders. This policy is shown by our steady growth as we are striving at all times to satisfy our customers with "HI-GRADE" MERCHANDISE, LOW PRICES AND EFFICIENT SERVICE.

DOGS, MONKEYS, CATS, RAEBITS, FANCY PIGEONS, JAPANESE WALTZING MICE

Write us your wishes—how old, what sex and color—and we will be pleased to quote you prices on same.

Dog and cat harness of every description. Write for prices.

We will buy all your birds and pets. Write us what you have.

CHICAGO BIRD AND CAGE COMPANY

THE FIRST WITH THE FINEST—WHITE CANARIES

No. 165.............................$17.00
Finished in beautiful two-tone colors of gold, green, brown. Has electric light.

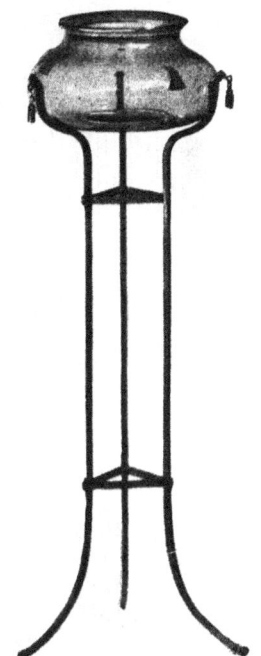

No. 10...............................$3.50
With 2 gallon crystal squat bowl. Finished in green, red or gold.

No. 270.............................$14.00
Finished in beautiful two-tone colors of gold, green, brown. Has electric light.

No. 355.............................$16.00
Finished in beautiful gold, green or brown with two-tone trim. Has electric flower.

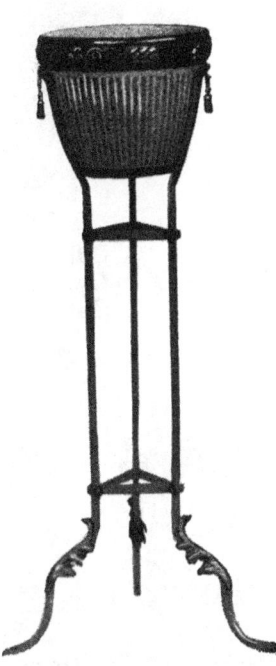

No. 20...............................$3.75
Finished in two-tone colors of green or red.

No. 154.............................$12.50
Finished in beautiful colors of gold, green or brown with two-tone trim. Has electric flower.

AQUARIUMS AND CASTLES

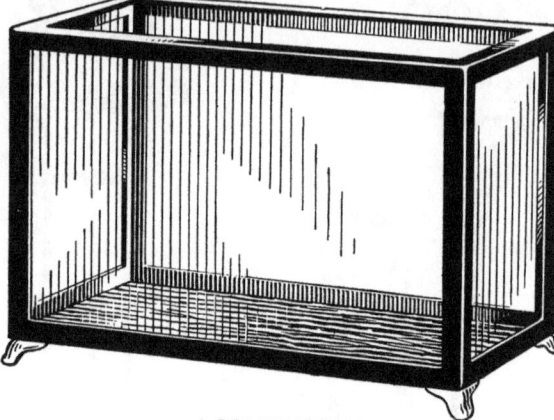

ROUND GLOBES

½ Gal	each	$0.40
1 Gal	each	.75
2 Gal	each	1.25
3 Gal	each	2.00

AQUARIUMS

No.	Long	Wide	High	Gal.	Price
01	9½	5½	6⅞	1	$3.00
01½	10½	6½	7⅝	1½	3.50
02	11½	7½	8¼	2	4.00
03	12½	8½	8⅝	3	4.50
04	13½	9½	9¼	4	5.00

Special sizes on request

SQUAT GLOBES

½ Gal	each	$0.45
1 Gal	each	.85
2 Gal	each	1.35
3 Gal	each	2.25

EGYPTIAN GLOBES

½ Gal	each	$0.50
1 Gal	each	.90
2 Gal	each	1.50

GLOBE AND AQUARIUM CASTLES

 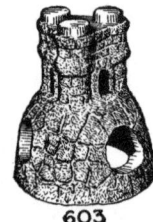  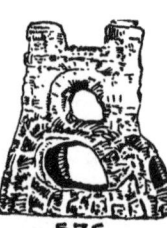 

596   603   597½   576   576½

Price ....15c   Price ....25c   Price ....50c   Price ....75c $1.00 to $1.50

CHICAGO BIRD AND CAGE COMPANY

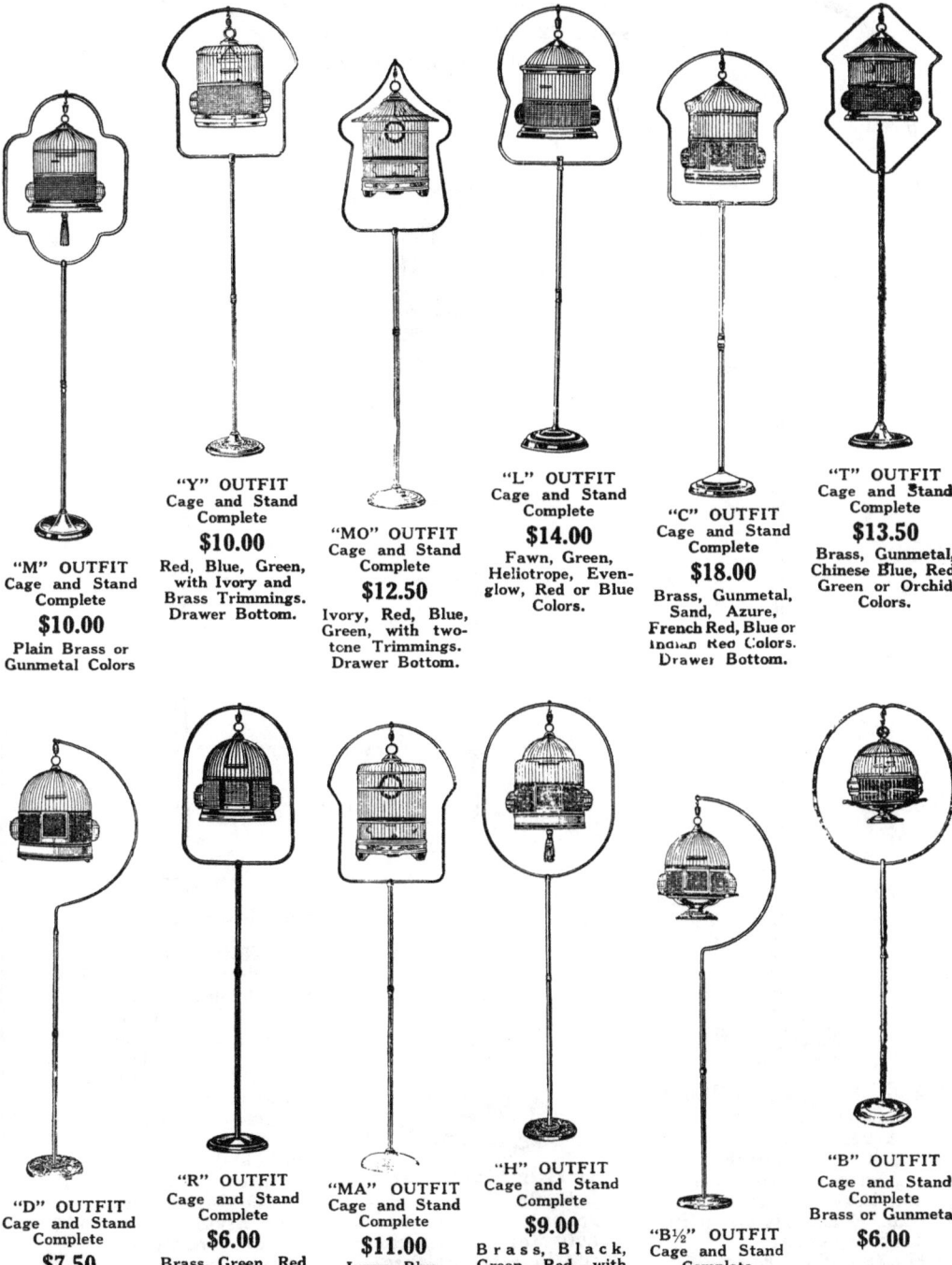

34 IF YOU ARE A MERCHANT OR DEALER, WRITE FOR PRICES

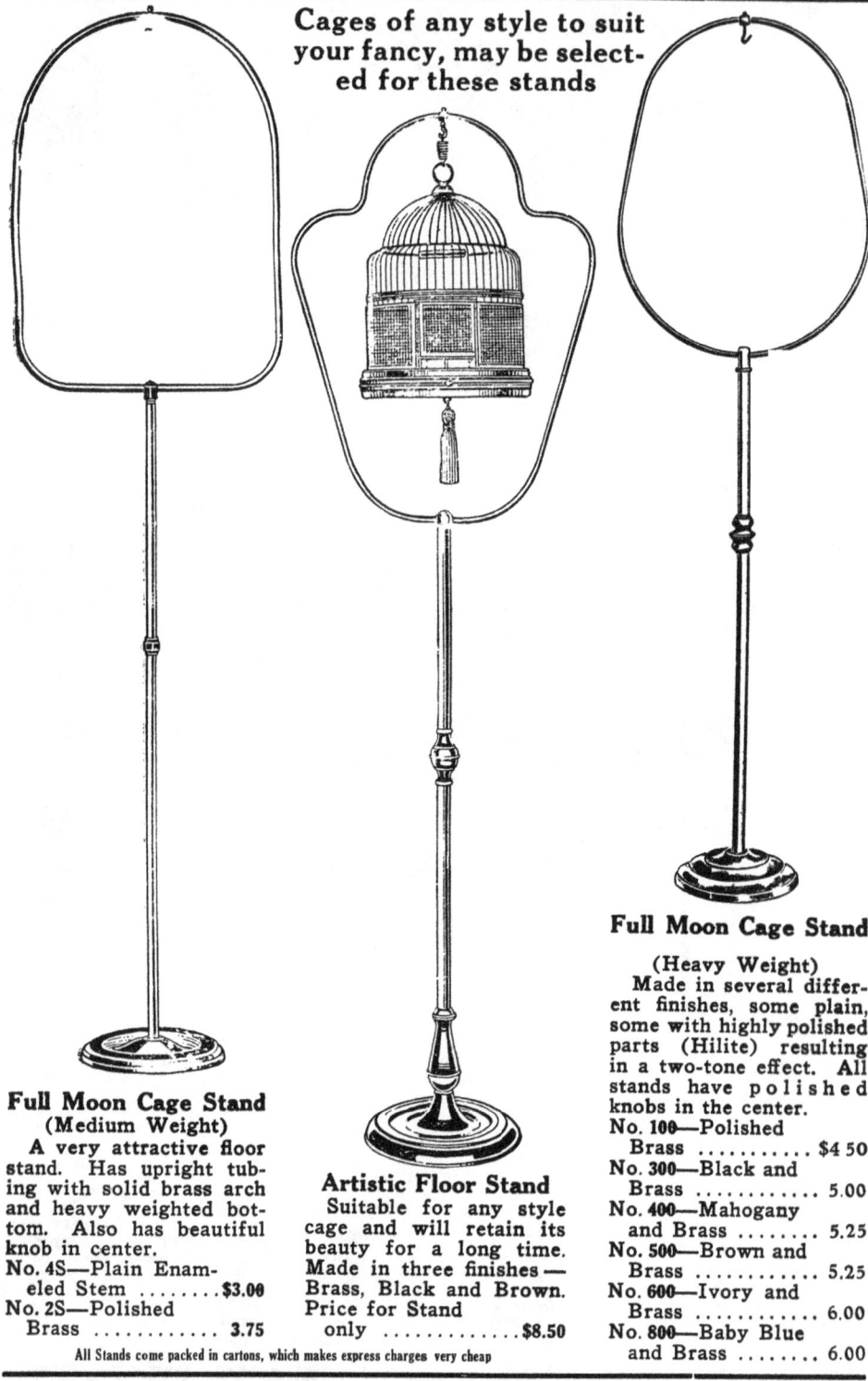

Cages of any style to suit your fancy, may be selected for these stands

Full Moon Cage Stand
(Medium Weight)

A very attractive floor stand. Has upright tubing with solid brass arch and heavy weighted bottom. Also has beautiful knob in center.

No. 4S—Plain Enameled Stem $3.00
No. 2S—Polished Brass 3.75

Artistic Floor Stand

Suitable for any style cage and will retain its beauty for a long time. Made in three finishes— Brass, Black and Brown. Price for Stand only $8.50

All Stands come packed in cartons, which makes express charges very cheap

Full Moon Cage Stand

(Heavy Weight)
Made in several different finishes, some plain, some with highly polished parts (Hilite) resulting in a two-tone effect. All stands have polished knobs in the center.

No. 100—Polished Brass $4.50
No. 300—Black and Brass 5.00
No. 400—Mahogany and Brass 5.25
No. 500—Brown and Brass 5.25
No. 600—Ivory and Brass 6.00
No. 800—Baby Blue and Brass 6.00

CHICAGO BIRD AND CAGE COMPANY

WE BUY AND SELL PETS—CANARIES, PARROTS, DOGS

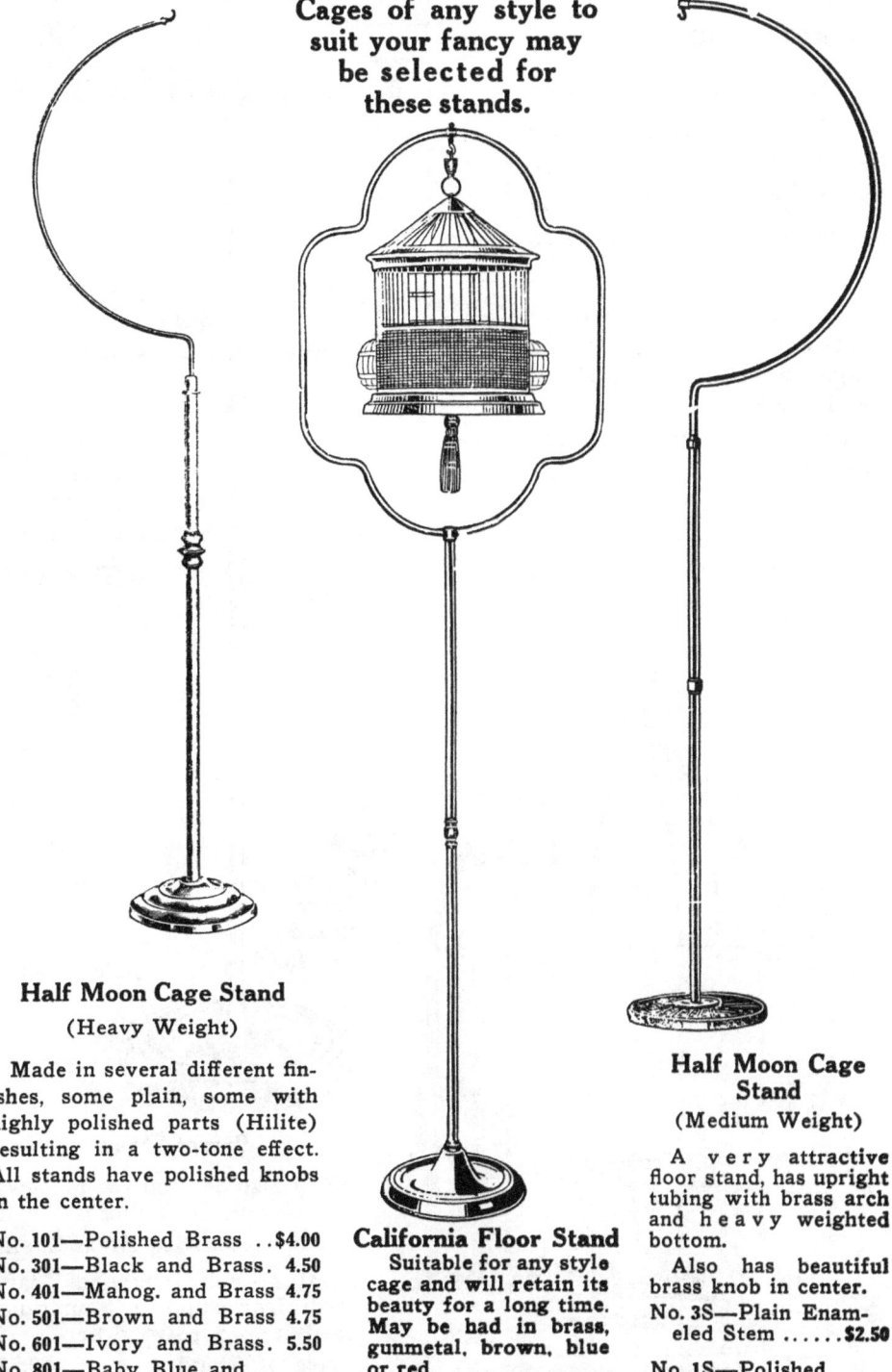

Cages of any style to suit your fancy may be selected for these stands.

Half Moon Cage Stand
(Heavy Weight)

Made in several different finishes, some plain, some with highly polished parts (Hilite) resulting in a two-tone effect. All stands have polished knobs in the center.

No. 101—Polished Brass .. $4.00
No. 301—Black and Brass. 4.50
No. 401—Mahog. and Brass 4.75
No. 501—Brown and Brass 4.75
No. 601—Ivory and Brass. 5.50
No. 801—Baby Blue and Brass 5.50

California Floor Stand

Suitable for any style cage and will retain its beauty for a long time. May be had in brass, gunmetal, brown, blue or red.
Price for Stand only $7.50

Half Moon Cage Stand
(Medium Weight)

A very attractive floor stand, has upright tubing with brass arch and heavy weighted bottom.

Also has beautiful brass knob in center.

No. 3S—Plain Enameled Stem $2.50

No. 1S—Polished Brass $3.25

CHICAGO BIRD AND CAGE COMPANY

ROUND PARROT CAGE

No. 01—12″ dia. $4.00
No. 02—13″ dia. 5.25
No. 03—14½″ dia. 7.00
No. 04—16″ dia. 8.50
No. 05—17½″ dia. 9.50

These cages have beautiful knobs and tin washers. Heavy hangers with brass nuts. Hardwood perches and swings. Heavy zinc bottoms. Tinned iron feed cups.

Fancy Parrot Stand
Price $15.00

Parrot Cover and Stand
Price $18.00

Parrot Stand
(May also be used for Macaws and Cockatoos)
Iron base, with Brass Shell.
Oval 24-inch Japanned Tray, with iron support aluminum feed cups, hardwood perch.
Price of Stand..........$9.50

CHICAGO BIRD AND CAGE COMPANY

SQUARE PARROT CAGES

PARROT CAGE

A parrot will usually talk more when confined to a cage. Every one who has a parrot should have a good cage even if they keep the bird the most of the time on a perch. Our cages are thoroughly well made, the wires being large and well tinned.

SQUARE PARROT CAGE

No. 035—15"x13". Ht., 24".....................$ 9.00
No. 037—17½"x15". Ht., 26"..................... 11.50

Brass top, tinned wire body, rail drilled and wires securely swaged, to increase strength of cage.

ROUND BRASS PARROT CAGES

This brass cage is a beautiful cage, both body and base being made of solid brass, finished bright and thoroughly lacquered to prevent tarnishing. Shaped the same as round parrot cage illustrated.
No. 02B—13" Dia. $10.00
No. 03B—14½" Dia. ... 12.00

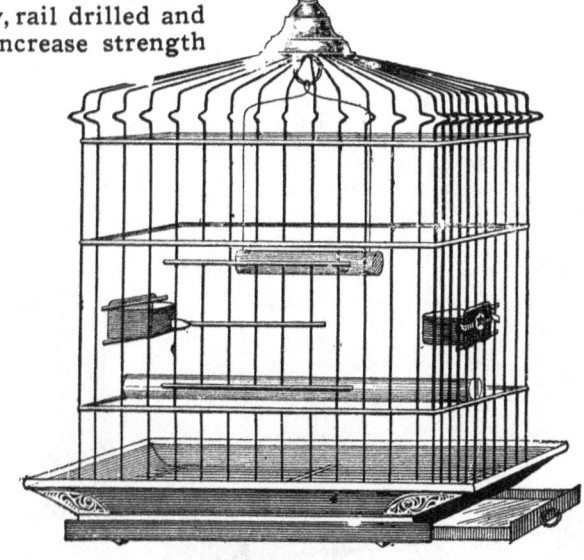

SQUARE PARROT CAGE

No. 35M—15"x13"x24" $12.00

No. 37M—17½"x15"x26" 14.00

Strongest parrot cages, constructed of steel wire, having cups, perches, swing, etc., wire grating, molding bottom and sliding tray.

CHICAGO BIRD AND CAGE COMPANY

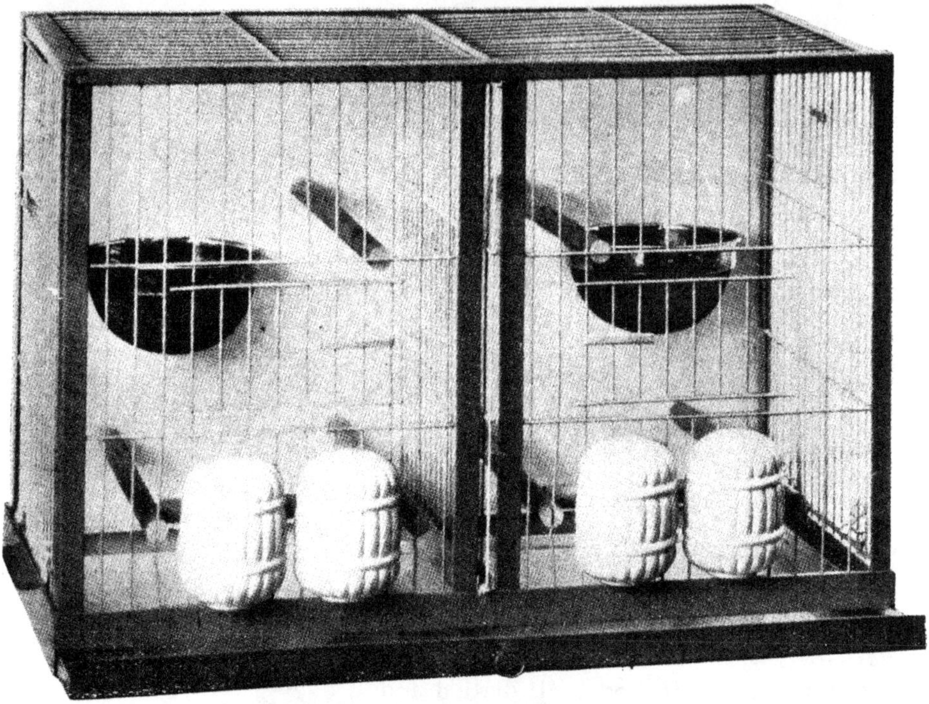

THE LARGER THE CAGE, THE BETTER THE BREEDING

JAPANNED BREEDING CAGE
Enameled, Vermin Proof

These cages are without doubt the strongest, most serviceable and attractive breeding cages made. They are trimmed in green, have solid and wire partitions, removable metal drawers and closed back. 4 glass cups, 6 perches and 2 nests.

No. 140—Medium Size, 18"x10"x12" high $6.00
No. 141—Medium Large Size, 20"x11"x13" high 7.25
No. 142—Large Size, 22"x12"x14" high 8.25

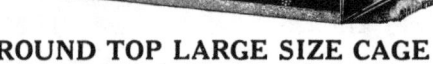

ROUND TOP LARGE SIZE CAGE

For Red Birds, Mocking Birds, Shana Thrushes. A real flying cage for all birds, young birds. Durable all metal. Enameled vermin proof.

No. 83—20¼"x12"x20" $7.50
No. 84—22½"x13"x21" 8.50
No. 85—24" x14"x23" 9.50

SINGLE BREEDING CAGES

Strongest constructed steel wire hardwood frame, breeding cages, possessing cups, perches and having a sliding drawer, enabling one to clean with ease.

No. 1B—14"x8½"x11" $3.00
No. 2B—16"x9" x11" 3.50
No. 3B—18"x10" 12" 3.75

Extra sizes made to order.

A ROOMY CAGE IS A HAPPY HOME FOR CANARIES 39

ENAMELED SINGLE BREEDING CAGES

No. 23—16"x9"x11" $3.75
No. 22—16"x10"x13½" 4.75

These cages may be used for all purposes such as breeding cages, flying cage for young birds, for aviary, for wild birds, etc.

ENAMELED BREEDING CAGE

No. 20—17½"x10¼"x12" $5.50
No. 21—20"x12"x16" 6.50

Strongest constructed metal frame, breeding cages with partition, possessing cups, perches and having sliding drawer, enabling one to clean with ease.

DOUBLE BREEDING CAGE

Strongest constructed steel wire hardwood frame, breeding cages with partition, possessing cups, perches and having sliding drawer, enabling one to clean with ease.

No. 4B—Double Breeding Cage, with partition, 17½"x11"x12½". Price..$4.50

No. 5B—Double Breeding Cage, with partition, 23"x13"x12". Price 5.50

Extra sizes made to order.

Wooden   *Wire*

OUTSIDE NEST BOARDS

Used for the outside of a breeding or any other cage. Our wire nests illustrated fit in perfectly. Very sanitary.

Wooden. Price 50c
Wire. Price 75c
Wooden. Per dozen.......... $5.00
Wire. Per dozen................ 7.00

CHICAGO BIRD AND CAGE COMPANY

40 QUALITY IS REMEMBERED LONG AFTER PRICE IS FORGOTTEN

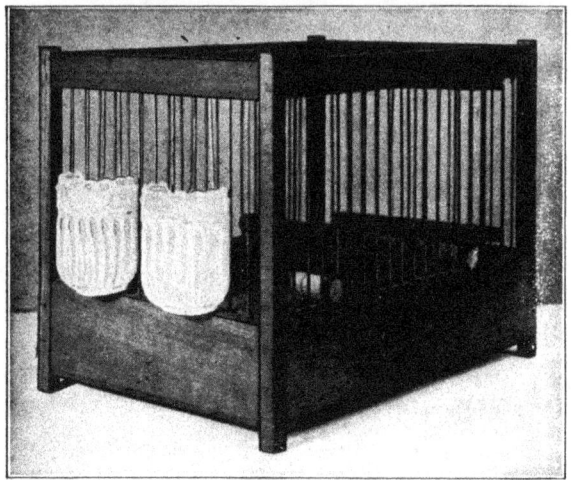

WIRE NESTS

No. 2N   No. 1N

Wire nest with swivel, 4 inches; vermin-proof; adapted to all breeding cages and nest boards.
Price 1N 15c
Price 2N 25c

BIRD NESTING

Bird nesting prepared of deer's hair, moss and other materials for birds to build their nests with.
Per package 10c
Twelve packages 70c

TRAINING CAGES

No. 1T—9¼"x6¼"x8" $0.90
In Dozen Lots........................ 9.00

Constructed wood and copper wire; has galvanized sliding drawer bottom. With cups, 20c extra.

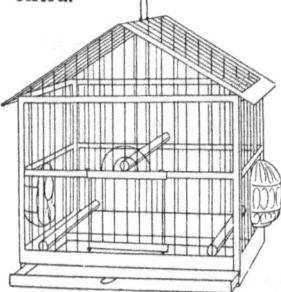

TRAINING CAGE OR SHELF CAGE
No. 2T

6½"x7½"x9" $1.00
In Dozen Lots ...10.00
Fitted with perches. Has sliding drawer with cups, 20c extra.

ENAMELED BUNGALOW CAGE
No. 24

10x8x13 in. $2.75
Three finishes: White enamel with either green or blue trimmings, also pure white.

ENAMELED TRAINING CAGE

Fitted with cups, perches, has sliding drawer and is white enameled.

No. 3T—10"x7¼"x9½"....$2.00

In Dozen Lots 21.00

TRAVELING CAGE
No. 4T

7¼"x5½"x5⅛" $1.50
Furnished with cups, perches and sliding tray.

CHICAGO BIRD AND CAGE COMPANY

WE CANNOT LIST EVERYTHING, WRITE US YOUR WISHES 41

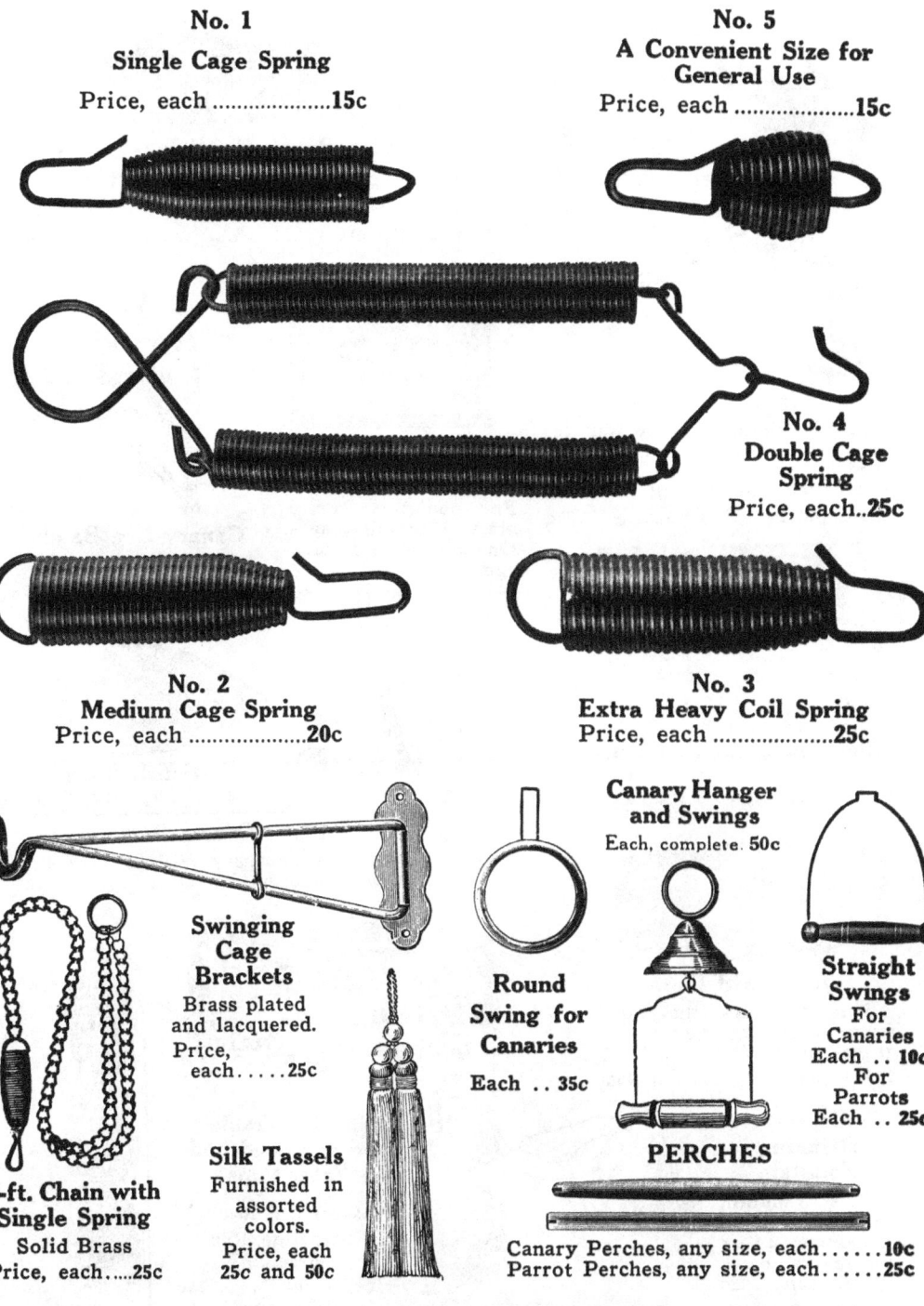

No. 1
Single Cage Spring
Price, each **15c**

No. 5
A Convenient Size for General Use
Price, each **15c**

No. 4
Double Cage Spring
Price, each.. **25c**

No. 2
Medium Cage Spring
Price, each **20c**

No. 3
Extra Heavy Coil Spring
Price, each **25c**

Swinging Cage Brackets
Brass plated and lacquered.
Price, each..... **25c**

Canary Hanger and Swings
Each, complete. **50c**

Round Swing for Canaries
Each .. **35c**

Straight Swings
For Canaries
Each .. **10c**
For Parrots
Each .. **25c**

2-ft. Chain with Single Spring
Solid Brass
Price, each..... **25c**

Silk Tassels
Furnished in assorted colors.
Price, each
25c and **50c**

PERCHES

Canary Perches, any size, each...... **10c**
Parrot Perches, any size, each...... **25c**

Kindly Include Postage With Your Remittance When Ordering Supplies. See Page 45

CHICAGO BIRD AND CAGE COMPANY

42 NO CASH REFUND BUT WILL GLADLY MAKE EXCHANGES

Training Whistle
This Training Whistle imitates the song of a canary perfectly. It produces sweet, musical notes, and is excellent for training canaries. Brass plated. Price..........35c

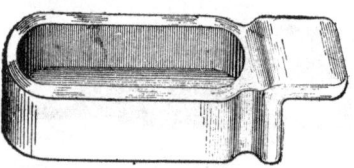

Opal Food Holder
TREAT CUP
For feeding eggs, dainties, etc.
Price, each..10c 3 for..25c

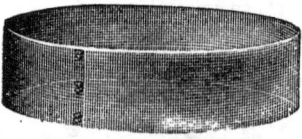

Wire Guard Cloth
This prevents the bird from scattering seed or gravel on the floor.
Price, per foot..........45c

Crystal Drinking Fountain
This fountain will provide drinking water for several days.
Price, each...95c

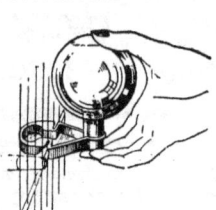

Lice Powder and Gun
To blow powder into every part of the cage and through the bird's feathers.
Price, complete 25c

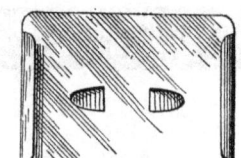

Cardholder Tin Plate
For pedigree. Price, etc. Fits all cages. One dozen in a package.
Price, per pkg.....90c

Canary Leg Bands
Numbers 1 to 100.
Price, per doz....$0.30
Price, per 100....... 1.95

Cuttlefish Bone
Price.....5c, 10c and 15c

Brass Charm Bell
To amuse your canary. Will fit any cage. Complete with holder, each.........20c

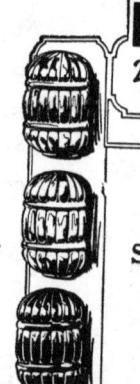

Non-Breakable Sanitary Seed and Water Cups
Assorted colors: White, Blue, Red, Green.
Price, each........25c

Kindly Include Postage With Your Remittance When Ordering Supplies. See Page 45.

CHICAGO BIRD AND CAGE COMPANY

OUR TRADE MARK "HI-GRADE" BRAND IS YOUR PROTECTION 43

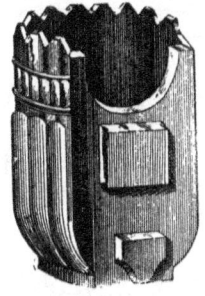

Tulip Cups
Fits all cages. Opal or crystal glass.
Price, each 15c
Two for 25c

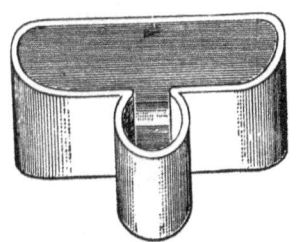

Single Point Cups
Price, each 15c

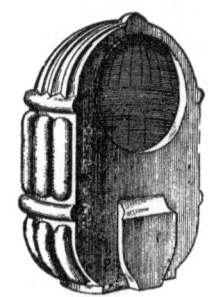

Shell Cups
Fits all cages. Opal or crystal glass.
Price, each 15c
Two for 25c

Inside Cup
No. 3C..........25c

German Imported Inside Cups
No. 1C....35c   No. 2C....25c

Inside Cup
No. 4C 20c

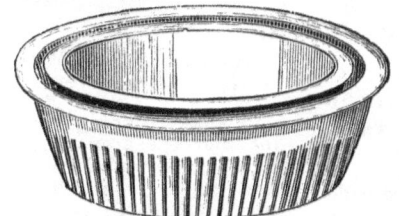

Shipping Cups
Price, each 25c

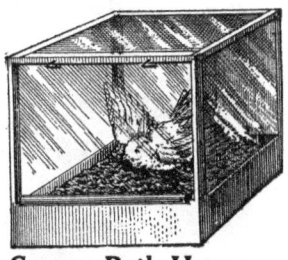

Canary Bath House
No. 1BH—White $0.75
No. 2BH—Red 1.00
No. 3BH—Green 1.00
No. 4BH—Blue 1.00
No. 5BH—Brass 1.25

Outside Canary Bath House
Something new. Will fit any canary cage. To be hung above door.
Price 75

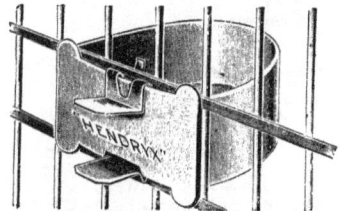

Canary Bath Dishes
Made of opal glass. Your bird should have a bath regularly.
Price, small...15c   Price, large...25c

Parrot Cups
Tinned Cast Iron.
Square Cage 50c
Round Cage 45c

Kindly Include Postage With Your Remittance When Ordering Supplies. See Page 45.

CHICAGO BIRD AND CAGE COMPANY

"HI-GRADE" FOODS AND REMEDIES

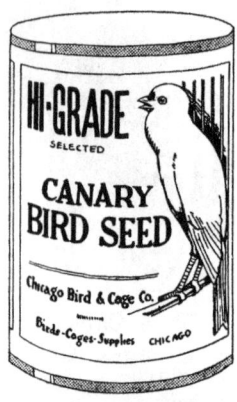

"HI-GRADE" BIRD SEED

This is a specialty with us and we sell tons of it. It is a mixture of the choicest Sicily Canary and German Sweet Rape. Its constant use will keep your bird in good song and best of condition.

Price, per Box........**20c**

"HI-GRADE" SONG RESTORER

For Canary Birds, and in fact, for all seed eating birds. This food not only keeps the bird in excellent condition, but being of a combination of alterative tonic seeds it acts on the bowels as well as the digestive organs, and thereby keeps disease away.

Price, per Can........**25c**

"HI-GRADE" BIRD GRAVEL

Birds have no teeth and to help them grind their food they must have gravel. Our "HI-GRADE" BIRD GRAVEL is the best for canaries and other birds. It should be sprinkled daily in the bottom of the cage.

Price, per Box........**15c**

"HI-GRADE" MOULTING FOOD

GUARANTEED to aid bird in getting over moult either in or out of season, quickly and normally restoring fine beautiful feathers and song at the same time.

Price, per Can........**25c**

"HI-GRADE" EGG BREAD Nestling & Mating Food

A very wholesome and highly nourishing food for mother birds during breeding. It will keep birds in perfect health, plumage and song, also to be fed to young baby birds.

Price, per Box........**15c**

"HI-GRADE" COLOR AND PEPPER FOOD

Invaluable during moulting and breeding period. Brings out that deep yellow color so much desired by bird fanciers. During breeding period, gives mother and young necessary nourishment and strength.

Price, per Can........**25c**

Kindly Include Postage With Your Remittance When Ordering Supplies. See Page 45.

CHICAGO BIRD AND CAGE COMPANY

WE SPECIALIZE IN BIRD FOODS AND PRODUCTS 45

"HI-GRADE" HEALTH FOOD

Eradicates impurities from the blood and restores to the songsters a strong and clear voice.

Price, per bottle......35c

"HI-GRADE" HEALTH BALL

Excellent for keeping birds in good health, plumage and song.

Price, each................15c
2 for 25c

"HI-GRADE" BIRD TONIC

This preparation is the best medicine for birds afflicted with asthma, colds and hard breathing. A real tonic for sick and weak birds.

Price, per bottle......25c

"HI-GRADE" CHARCOAL

This preparation is highly recommended as one of the best remedies for indigestion and other internal troubles of the cage birds.

Price, per can..........15c

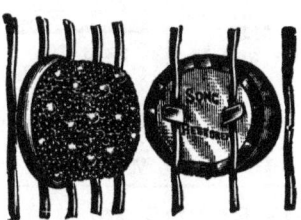

PEP

This is a bird food and medicine combined which is quite popular. The birds are fond of it. You will find this a very desirable item in the care and management of your bird.

Price, each................15c

"HI-GRADE" HEMP AND PEPPER

While too much hemp is fattening, a little hemp and pepper seed fed twice a week will keep your bird toned up and at the same time relish it.

Price, per Can.........25c

Kindly Include Postage With Your Remittance When Ordering Supplies. See Page 45.

CHICAGO BIRD AND CAGE COMPANY

BIG SAVINGS ON BIRD SEEDS AND SUPPLIES AT WHOLESALE

BIRD SEEDS AND SUNDRIES

"Hi-Grade" Mixed Bird Seed $0.20
  2 pkgs. 38c 3 pkgs. 52c Doz. pkgs. $1.80
"High-Grade" Bird Gravel .... .15
  2 pkgs. 28c 3 pkgs. 38c Doz. pkgs. $1.08
"Hi-Grade" Song Restorer .... .25
  2 pkgs. 46c 3 pkgs. 66c Doz. pkgs. $1.80
"Hi-Grade" Moulting Food .... .25
  2 pkgs. 46c 3 pkgs. 66c Doz. pkgs. $1.80
"Hi-Grade" Color and Pepper Food .... .25
  2 pkgs. 46c 3 pkgs. 66c Doz. pkgs. $1.80
"Hi-Grade" Egg and Nestling Food .... .15
  2 pkgs. 28c 3 pkgs. 38c Doz. pkgs. $1.30
"Hi-Grade" Bird Tonic .... .25
  2 pkgs. 46c 3 pkgs. 66c Doz. pkgs. $1.60
"Hi-Grade" Hemp and Peppers .... .25
  2 pkgs. 46c 3 pkgs. 66c Doz. pkgs. $1.60
"Hi-Grade" Health Food .... .35
  2 pkgs. 60c 3 pkgs. 85c Doz. pkgs. $2.88
"Hi-Grade" Health Ball .... .15
  2 pkgs. 25c Doz. pkgs. $1.20
"Hi-Grade" Pep .... .15
  2 pkgs. 28c 3 pkgs. 66c Doz. pkgs. $1.50
"Hi-Grade" Bird and Animal Salve .... .25
  2 pkgs. 27c 3 pkgs. 39c Doz. pkgs. $1.20
"Hi-Grade" Bird Bitters .... .35
  2 pkgs. 60c 3 pkgs. 85c Doz. pkgs. $2.85
"Hi-Grade" Charcoal .... .15
  2 pkgs. 27c 3 pkgs. 39c Doz. pkgs. $1.20
"Hi-Grade" Bird Nesting .... .10
  2 pkgs. 18c 3 pkgs. 24c Doz. pkgs. 70c
"Hi-Grade" Lice Powder and Gun .... .25
  2 pkgs. 46c 3 pkgs. 66c Doz. pkgs. $1.80
"Hi-Grade" Cuttlebone .... 5c, 10c and 15c
  Dozen pkgs., assorted sizes, 70c
"Hi-Grade" Wafer Fish Food .... .10
  2 pkgs. 18c 3 pkgs. 24c Doz. pkgs. 80c
"Hi-Grade" Natural Fish Food .... .15
  2 pkgs. 27c 3 pkgs. 39c Doz. pkgs. $1.00

BIRD SUPPLIES

Single Cage Springs $0.15
  2 pkgs. 27c 3 pkgs. 39c Doz. pkgs. 90c
Heavy Cage Springs .... .25
  2 pkgs. 46c 3 pkgs. 66c Doz. pkgs. $1.80
Double Cage Springs .... .25
  2 pkgs. 46c 3 pkgs. 66c Doz. pkgs. $1.80
Two Foot Chain with Spring .... .25
  2 pkgs. 48c 3 pkgs. 67c Doz. pkgs. $2.50
Training Whistles .... .35
  2 pkgs. 60c 3 pkgs. 95c Doz. pkgs. $2.95
Swinging Cage Bracket .... .25
  2 pkgs. 48c 3 pkgs. 67c Doz. pkgs. $2.20
Wire Nests, No. 1 .... .15
  2 pkgs. 29c 3 pkgs. 42c Doz. pkgs. $1.20
Wire Nests, No. 2 .... .25
  2 pkgs. 46c 3 pkgs. 66c Doz. pkgs. $1.80
Tulip Cups .... .15
  2 cups 25c Doz. cups $1.00
Shell Cups .... .15
  2 cups 25c Doz. cups $1.00
Single Point Cups .... .15
  2 cups 28c Doz. cups $1.20
Inside Cups .... .25
  2 cups 46c Doz. cups $2.20
German Cup No. 1C .... .35
  2 cups 60c Doz. cups $2.85
German Cup No. 2C .... .25
  2 cups 46c Doz. cups $2.40
Opal Food Holder .... .10
  3 pkgs. 25c Doz. pkgs. 75c
Canary Bath Dish, Small .... .15
  2 pkgs. 28c 3 pkgs. 39c Doz. pkgs. $1.20
Canary Bath Dish, Large .... .25
  2 pkgs. 46c 3 pkgs. 66c Doz. pkgs. $2.00
Outside Canary Bath House .... .75
  2 Houses $1.45 3 Houses $2.15 Doz. $7.50
Wire Guard Cloth, per foot .... .45

BIRD SEEDS IN BULK

The Best Money Can Buy—Airfanned—Double Recleaned

	Per Lb.	3 Lbs.	25 Lbs. or More
Mixed Bird Seed	$0.18	$0.50	$0.14
Sicily Canary Seed	.18	.50	.14
Large Sweet Rape Seed	.18	.50	.14
Hemp Seed	.16	.40	.10
Sunflower Seed	.20	.50	.15
Millett Seed	.15	.40	.10
Poppy Seed	.50	1.35	.40
Flax Seed	.20	.50	.15
Steel Cut Oats	.15	.40	.11
Lettuce Seed, Black	.50	1.35	.40
Lettuce Seed, White	.55	1.50	.45
Thistle Seed	.40	1.15	.35
Ground Canary Toast	.25	.65	.20
Hulled Oats	.20	.50	.16

All Seeds sold in any quantities desired, no matter how large or small. Write for special prices on larger quantities.

Kindly Include Postage With Your Remittance When Ordering Supplies. See Page 45.

CHICAGO BIRD AND CAGE COMPANY

EVERY CANARY WANTS ITS FOOD—"HI-GRADE"

"HI-GRADE" Now offers Canary Owners and Breeders the most complete line of scientifically prepared Bird Foods and Remedies on the market. Don't feed your bird injurious food when you can obtain a superior quality from us at a low price. Order a year's supply of bird seed, sundries, etc., and have it shipped by freight so as to save expenses. Always ADD POSTAGE when you order supplies to be shipped Parcel Post.

WHOLESALE

BIG SAVINGS ARE GAINED WHEN BUYING OUR COLLECTIONS. A REAL BARGAIN

OUR MEDICINE CHEST
Collection No. 1

1 Pkg. "Hi-Grade" Song Restorer	$0.25
1 Pkg. "Hi-Grade" Bird Tonic	.25
1 Pkg. "Hi-Grade" Bird Salve	.25
1 Pkg. "Hi-Grade" Supreme Health Ball	.15
1 Pkg. "Hi-Grade" Insect Powder	.25
1 Pkg. "Hi-Grade" Charcoal	.15
Total	$1.30
Special Collection Discount	.30
Our Price	$1.00
Weight 1½ lbs.	

CANARY FOOD SUPPLY
Collection No. 2

3 Lbs. "Hi-Grade" Mixed Canary Seed	$0.50
1 Pkg. "Hi-Grade" Song Restorer	.25
1 Pkg. "Hi-Grade" Hemp and Peppers	.25
1 Pkg. "Hi-Grade" Cuttle Bone	.10
1 Pkg. "Hi-Grade" Bird Gravel	.15
1 Pkg. "Hi-Grade" Health Ball	.15
1 Pkg. "Hi-Grade" Pep	.15
1 Pkg. "Hi-Grade" Moulting Food	.25
Total	$1.80
Special Collection Discount	.50
Our Price	$1.30
Weight 8 lbs.	

ECONOMY FOOD COLLECTION
Collection No. 3

6 Lbs. "Hi-Grade" Mixed Canary Seed	$1.00
2 Boxes "Hi-Grade" Song Restorer	.50
2 Boxes "Hi-Grade" Moulting Food	.50
1 Pkg. "Hi-Grade" Health Ball	.25
2 Pkgs. "Hi-Grade" Insect Powder	.50
1 Pkg. "Hi-Grade" Bird Salve	.25
1 Pkg. "Hi-Grade" Hemp and Pepper	.25
1 Pkg. "Hi-Grade" Bird Tonic	.25
1 Pkg. "Hi-Grade" Color Food	.25
Total	$3.75
Special Collection Discount	.75
Weight 10 lbs. Our Price	$3.00

PARROT COLLECTION
Collection No. 4

1 Box "Hi-Grade" Mixed Parrot Seed	$0.50
3 lbs. "Hi-Grade" Sunflower Seed	.50
1 Box "Hi-Grade" Parrot Gravel	.15
1 Pkg. "Hi-Grade" Insect Destroyer	.25
1 Pkg. "Hi-Grade" Bird Tonic	.25
1 Pkg. "Hi-Grade" Bird Salve	.25
Total	$1.90
Special Collection Discount	.40
Our Price	$1.50
Weight 10½ lbs.	

PARCEL POST BRINGS THE PACKAGE TO YOUR VERY DOOR
A QUICK WAY TO FIGURE PARCEL POST CHARGES

Weight in pounds	Local	First, up to 50 miles	Second, up to 150 miles	Third, 150 to 300 miles	Fourth, 300 to 600 miles	Fifth, 600 to 1,000 miles	Sixth, 1,000 to 1,400 miles	Seventh, 1,400 to 1,800 miles	Eighth, over 1,800 miles
1	$0.07	$0.07	$0.07	$0.08	$0.09	$0.10	$0.11	$0.13	$0.14
2	.08	.08	.08	.10	.13	.16	.19	.23	.26
3	.08	.09	.09	.12	.17	.22	.27	.33	.38
4	.09	.10	.10	.14	.21	.28	.35	.43	.50
5	.09	.11	.11	.16	.25	.34	.43	.53	.62
6	.10	.12	.12	.18	.29	.40	.51	.63	.74
7	.10	.13	.13	.20	.33	.46	.59	.73	.86
8	.11	.14	.14	.22	.37	.52	.67	.83	.98
9	.11	.15	.15	.24	.41	.58	.75	.93	1.10
10	.12	.16	.16	.26	.45	.64	.83	1.03	1.22
11	.12	.17	.17	.28	.49	.70	.91	1.13	1.34
12	.13	.18	.18	.30	.53	.76	.99	1.23	1.46
13	.13	.19	.19	.32	.57	.82	1.07	1.33	1.58
14	.14	.20	.20	.34	.61	.88	1.15	1.43	1.70
15	.14	.21	.21	.36	.65	.94	1.23	1.53	1.82

CHICAGO   BIRD   AND   CAGE   COMPANY

AMERICAN BRAND
BIRD & FISH FOODS

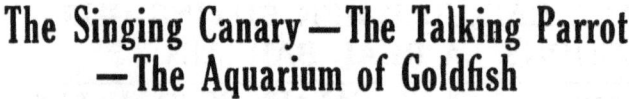

To the Lovers of the most Beautiful Home Pets in the World:

The Singing Canary — The Talking Parrot — The Aquarium of Goldfish

The American home is not complete without one or more of these beautiful pets. To help keep these little pets in their healthy condition you can absolutely depend upon the superior quality of our bird foods and remedies. As you know it is not safe feeding your pets anything but the very best and therefore we strongly recommend you to carefully select your bird supplies from this catalogue, as we have chosen the American Brand song and food preparations as the proper foods and remedies for your pets.

Look for the Singing Bird American Brand Food Products

HEALTH FOOD with COD LIVER OIL

This preparation is put up under the old reliable English Recipe for Birds that have lost their song, whether from the effects of moulting or otherwise. It is the only food to give immediate relief, and restore to the Songster a strong and clear voice. It eradicates impurities from and the blood, and by its use there will be a marked improvement in the song of all birds confined in cages.

Put up in hermetically sealed glass bottles.

Price, per bottle........35c   Per dozen........$3.00

SANITARY GRAVELPAPER
For the Busy Housewife—Convenient—Economical—Sanitary

A Dozen Sheets to a Package.

Square Cages		Round Cages	
9 x 9 inches oblong............25c		9 inches round................25c	
9 x11 inches oblong............25c		10 inches round................25c	
8½x11½ inches oblong............25c		11 inches round................25c	

CHICAGO BIRD AND CAGE COMPANY

LOOK FOR THE SINGING BIRD

Love Bird Seed
The properly blended mixture for all Love Birds or Paroquets. Packed in spout-top cartons for easy use.
Price, per box........25c

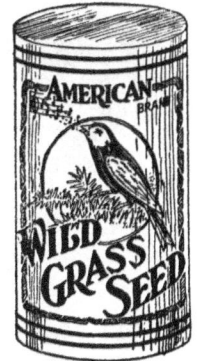

Wild Grass Seed
A selected variety of wild seeds, for all hard-bill Finches, such as European Siskins, Linnets, Saffron and African Finches. Also a treat for Canaries, when given twice weekly as a scratch food.
Price, per box........25c

Bird Grit
A combination of soluble minerals, gravel, crushed shells and charcoal. It can be used either with or in place of Bird Gravel. It is also packed in a spout-cover carton very convenient for use.
Price, per box.......15c

Bird Wash
An antiseptic to be placed in the bird's bath water. Will stop any skin disease by killing the germs. Also prevents mites.
It is nonpoisonous. Exceptionally good during hot weather. It fluffs the feathers and soothes the skin.
Price, per bottle...25c

Bird Books
"Feathered Pets, Their Care in Health and Disease" (illustrated). Each........35c
"Canary Breeding and Training." Each..............35c
"Parrots and Other Talking Birds" (illustrated). Each..........................35c
"Aquaria," illustrated book on goldfish and other aquarium fish. Each......35c

Catnip Mouse
A cloth filled with choice catnip leaves in the shape of a mouse. Give one to your cat and watch the fun. It acts as an exerciser, and makes the cat more playful.
Price, each 15c

Mixed Parrot Food
A perfectly blended mixture of seeds enjoyed by all parrots. Consists of sunflower, hemp, corn, pumpkin, monkey nuts, parrot peppers, peanuts, and polly bread.
Price, per box................40c

Parrot Tonic
Colds are more fatal to Parrots than any other disease. Colds can be prevented or cured by using Parrot Tonic as directed on bottle. It is a great aid when moulting.
Price, per bottle...25c

Bird Salve
A mild balm prepared for use on birds. Soothes and heals sore and scaly legs. Packed in ¼ oz. tin boxes.
Price, per can.....25c

CHICAGO BIRD AND CAGE COMPANY

A COMPLETE ASSORTMENT OF FISH FOODS

Wafer Fish Food
A prepared wafer fish food of finest quality.

Price, per box........10c

Aquarium Plants
Cabomba Moss $0.15
Myrio Phyllum Moss .15
Ludwich Moss ..... .20

Natural Fish Food
The most universally used fish food, finely ground, ready to feed. Contains shrimp and valuable mineral salts. Packed in sift-top cartons. Large size.

Price, per box........25c

Shrimp Fish Food
Used for fancy goldfish and tropicals. Finely ground and packed in tins.

Price, per can..........15c

Sea Sand
A white coarse gravel especially adapted to aquarium use, owing to the ease with which plants take root in it. Also very easy to clean.

Price, per box........20c

Natural Fish Food
The most universally used fish food, finely ground, ready to feed. Contains shrimp and valuable mineral salts. Packed in flat tin cans.

Price, per can........15c

Aquarium Shells
These shells are very ornamental.

Price, per box.............25c
Price, per lb...............35c

Ant Eggs
This excellent food is always satisfactory for turtles, larger goldfish, salamanders, toads, frogs, chameleons, small alligators, etc.

Price, per box.............25c

Fish Tonic
A fungus cure and tonic for all types of aquaria fish. Will quickly rid an aquarium of any fish disease. Used as a preventative once or twice a month, will keep fish in a healthy and contented condition.

Price, per bottle 15c

CHICAGO BIRD AND CAGE COMPANY

GOLD FISH AND SUPPLIES

No Fish or Moss Shipped During June, July or August

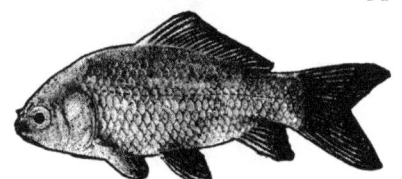

GOLD FISH

Small—1" to 1½"..................each **$0.10**
Medium small—1½" to 2" each   .15
Medium—2" to 2½"...........each   .20
Large—about 4" ....each   .25

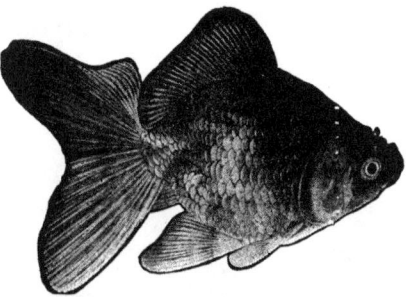

LONG TAIL COMET GOLD FISH

Has exceptionally long tail and fins

3" ....each **$0.30**
4" ....each   .35
5" to 6"........... ....each   .65
6" to 9"............. ....each **1.25**

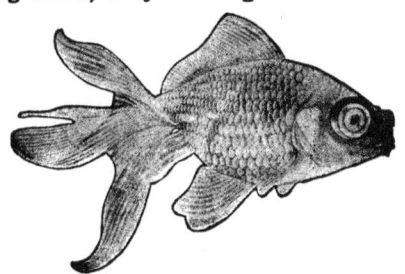

JAPANESE FANTAIL GOLD FISH

The most beautiful of aquaria fish. Have large double tails.
Small ....each **$0.50**
Medium ....each   .75
Large ....each **1.00**

CHINESE TELESCOPE GOLD FISH

Have large protruding eyes with plain and fan tail.
Each...............................**50c** to **$1.25**

Nets, with handle, each................**25c**

NOTE: All gold fish are shipped by express. When ordering fish send **25c** extra for shipping bucket.

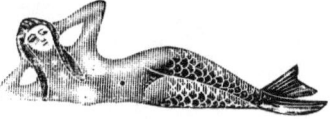

MERMAIDS

Assorted colors and sizes.
Prices..... **35c, 50c, 70c $1.00**

ORNAMENTS AND SUPPLIES

Fish Gravel, per box......................**25c**
Floating Ducks, each....**10c, 15c, 25c**
Sea Shells ....per box **25c**

"Aquaria," illustrated book on gold fish and other aquarium fish, each **35c**.

FISHER BOY

Very attractive, designed to sit on edge of aquarium or globe.
Complete with fish pole.
Price **75c, $1.00**

CHICAGO BIRD AND CAGE COMPANY

www.ingramcontent.com/pod-product-compliance
Lightning Source LLC
LaVergne TN
LVHW041500070426
835507LV00009B/714